PEEK-A-BOO

Numbers
and
Counting

Ruth Owen
Consultant: Jillian Harker

QEB Publishing

1 one

Good morning, Peek-a-boo!
There is **1 bed** in Peek-a-boo's room.
He has **1 teddy bear**.

Peek-a-boo has **only one** of some other things
in his room. Can you name them?

2 two

It's time for breakfast!

Peek-a-boo wants
2 pieces of toast.

There are **two** of some other things.
Can you spot them?

3 three

It's time to feed the pets.
Peek-a-boo has **3 carrots**
for the rabbits.

How many rabbits are there?

Can you count
Peek-a-boo's goldfish?

Does the puppy have
three dog biscuits?
How many does he have?

4 four

Peek-a-boo is washing the dishes.
He has washed **4 spoons**.

How many forks can you count?
Now count the dirty plates.

5

5 five

Mommy Penguin is doing the laundry.
She has **5 T-shirts** to wash.
Try to count them with her.

Which T-shirt has **5 spots** on it?

Can you count **five towels** on top of the washing machine?

6 six

Peek-a-boo is hanging socks on the clothesline.

Peek-a-boo has **6 clothespins** in his basket.

How many striped socks can you spot?

Count the red socks.

7 seven

Peek-a-boo is making a yummy fruit salad for lunch.

He has put **7 blueberries** in the bowl.

How many strawberries can you see?

Now count each of the other fruits.

8 eight

Peek-a-boo is playing with his building bricks. He has **8 bricks.**

Peek-a-boo loves to read!
Let's count Peek-a-boo's books.

9

9 nine

It's time for Peek-a-boo's bath!
Peek-a-boo has made **9 bubbles**.
Can you count them?

How many yellow ducks can you count?

10 ten

Peek-a-boo is wet from his bath.
He has made **10 puddles!**

Peek-a-boo chooses his pajamas.
How many pairs of pajamas
does Peek-a-boo have?

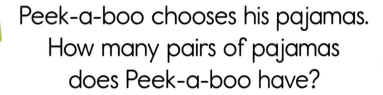

Look at this picture of
Peek-a-boo's living room.

Can you match the
things in the room
to the numbers **1** to **10**?

Peek-a-boo will help you
with the first one.

There is **1 television** in
Peek-a-boo's living room.

1 2 3 4

How many chairs are there in your living room?

5 6 7 8 9 10

13

It's Mommy Penguin's birthday.
Peek-a-boo is baking a birthday cake.

How many eggs does
Peek-a-boo have?

Let's count the cupcakes!

How many gingerbread penguins has Peek-a-boo made?

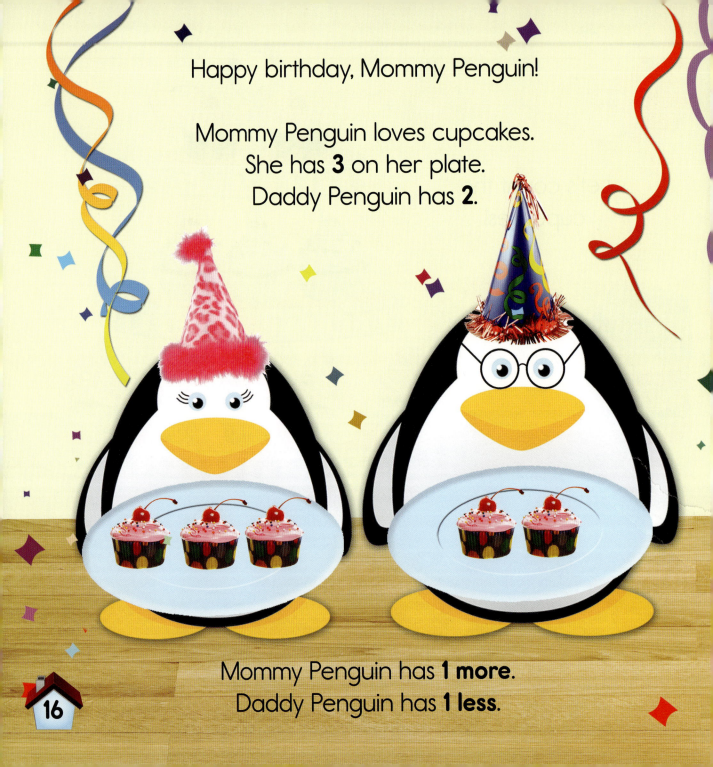

Happy birthday, Mommy Penguin!

Mommy Penguin loves cupcakes.
She has **3** on her plate.
Daddy Penguin has **2**.

Mommy Penguin has **1 more**.
Daddy Penguin has **1 less**.

Which bunch of balloons has **1 less**? Is it the blue bunch or the green bunch?

Which plate has **1 more**? Is it the plate of gingerbread penguins or the plate of blue cupcakes?

17

Look at the pictures of
Peek-a-boo's family.

Count the penguins in each picture.

Can you match each picture
to one of these numbers?

4 8 6 2 7 3

Peek-a-boo is practicing **more** and **less**.
Can you help him?

Count the groups of fruit.
Which has **1 less**?

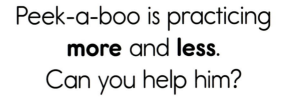

Count the groups of toys.
Which has **1 more**?

Count the groups of pets.
Which has **1 more**?

Count the groups of socks.
Which has **1 less**?

Let's play MATCH
with Peek-a-boo.

Peek-a-boo has two cards.
There are **5 ducks** on each card.
The cards are the **same**!

Now it's your turn.
Look at Peek-a-boo's cards.
Find two cards that are the **same**.

When you find them,
shout "Peek-a-boo MATCH!"

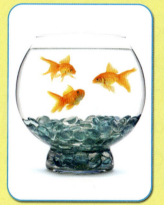

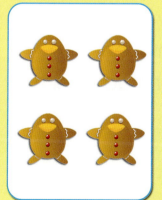

More fun with Peek-a-boo!

Now look back through your book. Let's do some more counting with Peek-a-boo!

How many **teddy bears** can you count in your book?

Peek-a-boo loves blue cupcakes! Count all the **blue cupcakes** in your book.

How many **presents** did Mommy Penguin have at her birthday party?

1 2 3 4 5

Look around your bedroom. What things do you have **one** of?

Can you count the **green socks** on Peek-a-boo's clothesline?

How old are you? Match your age to one of the big red numbers.

Look at Peek-a-boo's fruit salad. Does he have **more** orange slices than apples?

Now look at Peek-a-boo's living room. Which chair has **1 less** spot?

6 7 8 9 10

Notes for parents and teachers

The activities in this book are designed to introduce children to the important concepts of numbers and counting. The emphasis is on making learning fun, by using an engaging character to capture and focus the interest of young children. The book will help children learn how to count small groups of items and recognize numerals up to 10.

Sit with the child and read each page to them. Allow time for the child to think about the activity. Encourage them to talk about what they are doing as they carry out the activity. Praise all attempts. If the child is hesitant, show the child how to begin by demonstrating the first part of the activity yourself.

Remember to keep activities short and to make them fun. Stop while your child is still interested. Avoid times when your child is tired or distracted, and try again another day. Children learn best when they are relaxed and enjoying themselves. It's best to help them experience new concepts in small steps, rather than do too much at once.

Use the book as a starting point for activities that your child could carry out at home or when you are out together. Some ideas that you could try are:

- Play "Where's Peek-a-boo?" after each activity.

- Encourage your child to help you set the table, counting out items of forks, spoons, and knives.

- Play counting games when you are out together. By asking for only red cars or square signs to be counted, you will keep numbers small and reinforce other important concepts.

- Suggest that your child make a picnic for a group of toys, counting out the pieces of "food" as they make it.

- Write the numerals 1 to 10 on pieces of paper. Play "Go fetch," asking your child to bring you that number of toys, books, etc. Then let your child use the cards to give you instructions and check if you have counted your items correctly.

Created by: Ruby Tuesday Books
Designer: Emma Randall

Copyright © QEB Publishing, Inc. 2011

Published in the United States by
QEB Publishing, Inc.
3 Wrigley, Suite A
Irvine, CA 92618

www.qed-publishing.co.uk

Library of Congress Cataloging-in-Publication Data
Owen, Ruth, 1967-
Numbers and counting / Ruth Owen ; consultant:
Jillian Harker.
    p. cm. -- (Peek-a-boo penguin)
ISBN 978-1-60992-056-2 (library binding)
1. Mathematics--Study and teaching (Primary)
2. Education, Preschool--Activity programs. I. Title.

QA135.6.O89 2012
513.2'11--dc22

2011004052

ISBN: 978-1-60992-193-4 (saddlestitched)

Printed in China